What I Remember Most Is Everything

Sharon Tracey

Copyright © 2017 by Sharon Tracey
ALL CAPS PUBLISHING
All rights reserved.

ISBN 978-0692836705
(ALL CAPS PUBLISHING)

Cover Design: Kelly Tracey Hird

for Kelly, Will, and Sam

Contents

Arrival

To the City on a Hill / 3

California

My Closet / 9
School of Violet / 10
Between Earth and Sky / 11
Legs on a Bench in North Beach / 12
Searching for Work / 13
Muni Bus on Geary / 14
Searching for Saint Francis / 15
Tangerines and Turquoise / 18
Two Water Glasses / 19
Walking Up 24th Street from BART / 20
Highway Meditation / 21
Along the Sacramento River / 22
Confluence / 23
California City / 24
Pacific Coast Highway & Santa Monica / 25
Opalescence / 26
Maybe Just This / 27
What I Remember Most Is Everything / 28

Counterpoints

Color, Memory / 31
Speak, Color / 32

Compositions

Red Square / 37
Dear Matisse / 38
Artist and Goldfish / 39
van Gogh's Red Vineyard / 40
Road with Cypress and Star / 41
The Water Lilies at Giverny / 42
Portal in the Sun / 43
Two Blue Riders / 44
Composition with Saints / 46
Separation in the Evening / 47
Mourning Breakfast / 48
Girl with Red Bow / 49
Morandi Still Life: Cat and Five Objects / 50
Natura Morta / 51
The Work of Gray / 52
I Was So Small I Saw So Much / 53
The Green Fuse / 54

Travel

Two Suitcases / 57
Yukon Gold / 58
Sunday in Sicily / 60
Saint Petersburg / 62
The Spanish Steps / 63
Black Forest Walk / 64
What Light Can Do / 65
Munich Was Radiant / 66
Knitting in the Dark / 68

List of Things Left I Will Come Back For / 69
Desire Path / 70
Sparring Time / 71
We Made the Rain / 72

Return

Climbing the Seven Hills / 75

Notes on the Artists / 79
Acknowledgements / 83
About the Author / 85

Colors produce a corresponding spiritual vibration ...

—Wassily Kandinsky, *Concerning the Spiritual in Art*

What I Remember Most Is Everything

ARRIVAL

To the City on a Hill

*Washington D.C. > Pittsburgh > Toledo > Chicago >
Omaha > Salt Lake City > Reno > San Francisco*

Twenty-one, solo and climbing the Greyhound steps
with a backpack, 500 dollars and paints
and a one-way-USA-anywhere ticket heading out west

I will stay for ten years but I don't know this yet

a bus is not a sub, thank God we have real air in here
the faint smell of disinfectant will diffuse in a few hours
the windows fogged with passenger breath will finally clear

my daughter will ride her own bus but I don't know this yet

listen as the door squeaks shut like a giant squeegee, breathe in
and swallow the marshmallow sky on this migration west
count the green highway signs in Helvetica as we speed past

*the single mom who boards in Pittsburgh will want to talk
but I don't know this yet*

sometimes we stop to rest and surprising birds appear
as in Toledo, Ohio where a yellow-bellied woodpecker
and a scarlet tanager nibble insects in plain sight on the curb

I will be the only girl traveling alone but I don't know this yet

at midnight the bus stops in Chicago so we exit to stretch—
groggy from little sleep and too many overheard conversations,
the tones droning on, knowing more than we should

there will be words and forgiveness but I don't know this yet

wheat fields rise in waves all morning until we reach Omaha
at noon where a rock band is playing near the depot and
the mother from Pittsburgh wonders why anyone travels alone

after three days the body will ache but I don't know this yet

cornflowers crop up in clusters along the highway as we cross
into Colorado and I try to concentrate on their true blueness
but the man from Shanghai heading to Fresno cannot stop
talking about the lack of roasted shell peanuts on the East Coast

there will be an epidemic and heartbreak but I don't know this yet

with a four-hour layover in Salt Lake City we visit the shining
Mormon temple and mill about in alabaster air with a ragtag
collection of tourists and worshippers and still have time
for a Coke, a pretzel and a postcard

I will miss four sisters and have a fifth but I don't know this yet

speeding into Nevada the sky turns bile green as thunderheads
boil then rinse the highway and at the next stop a boy of eighteen
boards and sits across the aisle, same name as my brother John,
same name as my grandfather, same as the Apostle John

*same name as my future husband—father-to-be of two sons—
but I don't know this yet*

the high desert shimmers as tumbleweeds spin past us
and there is no more water until the next stop in Reno
and I think of Jesus's words—*I am the light of the world*

there will be leaving and returning but I don't know this yet

as the bus crosses into California there is a sudden jolt
as the driver guns the gas and we roll on and the fog rolls in
and the bus finally reaches San Francisco and pulls into
the depot near Folsom Street and emits us to time

there will be a clinging to color but I don't know any of this yet

CALIFORNIA

My Closet

After all these years
open the closet door, closest

to the bay window, still
hanging there, spare—

the purple jumpsuit, the pink
pants, the floral watercolor dress,
necklaces of venetian glass—

let the clothes talk so we can
walk, quiet up the loud hills
and down the hall to my desk

to the sun shining on
the blue-lined paper
in the black notebook

the words unfinished
in the middle of a sentence.

School of Violet

In case it won't be clear—
I'm from the school where violet rules—

not violent, not volatile
not purple—a mere mixture of red and blue—

but the school with the highest vibration
in the visible spectrum

where we're prone to prayer
and the month of September

more to embers than to fire,
content on occasion to be invisible

till shadows have their say
late afternoons

and there you'll find us

schoolgirls on our knees in the grass
picking violets.

Between Earth and Sky

That first night in San Francisco we fell
in love, bought a gallon of milk and walked
to the wake for your uncle killed in his kitchen
earlier in the week and we met a girl
named Josie who sang in the gospel choir
at Glide Church near Geary who knew
many of those who died in Jonestown
and that fall White shot and killed Milk
and Moscone at City Hall on a dim Monday
morning and there was the trip to Yosemite
in the Sierras where you drove your Mustang
head-on into the black Jeep while reading
the topographic map so we went flying
and found ourselves looking up into the faces
of giants—those Sequoias so Evergreen
and wearing the sequins of the sun
who took their prickly hands to skin
skim milk blue and limb to limb
cracked open the shining place
between earth and sky
where the dead are no longer dead
but are still sleeping it being early
and we dreamed thinner and dimmer
thoughts until they needled us
and sent us on our way back down
the divided highway while they
went deeper into heavenly blue
to the beginning, when we looked back.

Legs on a Bench in North Beach

Can legs disappear just like that—
stretched out in a violet pool
sixty seconds strong,
shimmering then gone?

Like a canopy of bright leaves
shimmers, then shakes loose
its rusted stars.

Searching for Work

Back when we used yellow pages
mine were worn
soft as corn silk,
my purple sleeves

as I searched through them
scanning subjects
for steady work,
then drifted back

to Steinbeck's *Grapes of Wrath*
the Dust Bowl trek
salted light,
migrants heading west.

Muni Bus on Geary

Bracelets of blue silver
snaked up both arms and she
blind, was singing a show tune
to a plumed bird
on the shirt of a boy
in the seat in front of us
who had turned
to listen.

The driver—suddenly blinded
by sun—swerved
to miss the moving
van that ran the red light
right in front of us
its left side stenciled
in bright blue letters
spelling
BREAD PARADISE
but the *B*
was missing.

Searching for Saint Francis

i.

It's another holy week and I'm reading the missile
in Mission Dolores on 16th Street
and it's early Monday morning
the sun a warm sandstone
and there is a yellow heat on Mission
the sweet smell of mangos
and the boys at the corner market
are plucking corn like guitars
and the old women are fondling
the thin-skinned oranges
and I'm sitting in the sixth pew
praying for rain
and some deliverance
as Saint Francis of Assisi
has promised to meet me
so I wait and watch
the oatmeal sky
outside the window
and he said be patient
but he is late and I have work
so I depart for the bus stop
a brush of wind against
the flowers on my dress
drawing light like butterflies.

ii.

Across the street at the teal-trimmed laundromat
a tall man near the open door
is folding jeans with giant
spade-like hands, gathering up
then doubling them again
into perfect pleated stacks
and on the corner of Dolores
one man is preaching with long, beautiful fingers
one man is reading every page of the newspaper equally
one man is drinking red wine from a green bottle
as the bus pulls up with its hiss
and we board and pass Peña's barbershop
and Chris's hamburger place
with the home-fried chips and catch
bites of conversations
and everyone seems hungry
as we disembark for work.

iii.

Now it's the hour when the sky has washed
the colors from her hair and left us
at our usual spot—Little Joe's on Columbus—
us and the city on Saturday night
and we've ordered the usual—cacciucco
and Joe is singing *amore* behind the counter
the flames flaring above the black pans

and the cooks are cracking jokes like eggs
and a crowd has lined up outside
the plate glass window
and they're laughing, making
their own steam as they wait
just up the street from City Lights
and the bands are warming up
at the Stone on Broadway
and it seems the whole world
is out walking the city streets
tonight in search of something—
tourists, winos, lovers and runners—
tomorrow being the third Sunday
in May, *Bay to Breakers* race day
where there will be costumed teams
of centipedes, clowns and human bees—
and Joe brings over our steaming bowls
of fish stew with plenty of Italian bread
and pours more chianti and later
we will drink espresso at Caffé Trieste
on Vallejo and tomorrow will rise
early and put on our sneakers
and head to the starting line on Howard
and I will finally meet Saint Francis
in the crowd and hear voices
and will run with the poets on the streets.

Tangerines and Turquoise

Tangerines and turquoise

go together

the way a body part

can be stuck or grafted

to another like a tree

growing soft

and then hard

the way carrots can color

the skin orange

or the sun colors

the sky turquoise

the way tangerines fill

this turquoise bowl

appearing

then

disappearing.

Two Water Glasses

sit at Mario's Bohemian Cigar Store Café
corner of Columbus and Union

debating how long they can
stay at our table, full of water

fifteen days at most, maybe
before they will evaporate

leaving just silica, soda and lime
and the thick dust

will begin to stick
and they may last a million years.

How minerals color glass—
    gold's red   copper's blue   iron's chrome green

seems a small miracle

shattering with ease
but even broken, everlasting

neither liquid nor solid
but some state in-between.

Walking up 24th Street from BART

Two tiger swallowtails   fly
fan fast the green flowers

in a green garden just past Octavia
where I pause to listen:

a burly boy and a green girl
stand arguing in the spiked grass

blustery at first, then quiet
as a weed pulled soft in damp earth

I watch them: girl, boy, butterflies
the slight breeze between their legs and wings

still flower-pressed against my eye

Highway Meditation

The bus broke down near Exit 10

there was nowhere to go
nothing to do but wait

and watch with wistful eyes
the highway hurling cars.

We climbed down, then stood around

as rain came sudden
in the summer heat

and the sun crackled through
the black-green trees

spreading silhouettes across
our asphalt feet.

We stood around, then bent down

emptying our minds
like tipped bowls

and watched the dusk
wet and blinking

drink the last of the light.

Along the Sacramento River

Trilling over pebbled toes, she opened
        her mouth wide at our feet

and how could you not love that?

At dusk she wore her armor lightly
        against the sun's face

and early next morning spread
        a green glaze for breakfast

her sediments pouring right through us
        in the elbow of her oxbow.

Can you see the row of sycamores dropping
        gold leaves on her skin?

Muffled hearts, one of us dove in.

Confluence

> *...that is the composition of the time in which each lives*
> — Gertrude Stein

the way two great rivers flow
        milk green to yellowed light

their gradients approaching juncture
        the punctured swirl of union

the way a flame-red sunbird
        perched in light dazzles

then becomes hidden
        in shaded brambles

eyes composing time
        the colliding

roiling rivers // middens // bidden birds

California City

plus 28 more paintings by Wayne Thiebaud

Travelers . Circle street . Coming and going .
      Bakery lady . White shoe .
      Girl with pink hat .

Two streets down . Two seated figures .
      Brown river . River turns .
      Green river lands .

Road through . Orange grove .
      Lake edge . Delta water .
      Dark ridge and clouds .

Sunset streets . Uphill streets .
      Intersection . Heavy traffic .
      Cat and building .

Woman with yellow hat . Window table .
      Standing man . Violin and shadow .
      Watermelon and knife .

Robed woman with letter . Dark lipstick .

Pacific Coast Highway & Santa Monica

plus 22 more paintings by David Hockney

Mulholland Drive: The road to the studio .
    Cactus with lemons . Blue hydrangeas .
    Rubber ring floating in a swimming pool .

The other side . The sea at Malibu .
    Three green waves with orange sand .
    A bigger splash .

The only one with waves . Henry .
    Walking past two chairs .
    Green tide . Potted jade .

Play within a play . The photographer
    and his daughter . Self portrait in mirror .
    Red and black fruit .

Three sunflowers and a bottle of water .
    A lawn being sprinkled .
    Light and dark getting together .

The railing . Divine .

Opalescence

The day my love walked
out the door—no word
no warning, just gone—

hungry for what I knew not
I pulled a book off the shelf
thumbing through worry

the *Life of Minerals* I read
how gems can craze—

internally crack at random
if dried too rapidly
or exposed to strobes
the sudden pause—

how something hard
as an opal holds
water ten percent

trapped invisibly
like a vitreous eye
flashing
pinfire pearls

Can we howl at something please

Maybe Just This

A white piano in a black room
in a house overlooking the Pacific
on Bodega Bay, you play
your composition, we listen

cannot even hear the broken key
we soon swallow the sound
and submit to the sea
hairs on skin spiked like urchins

the moon rising like a sickle strung
to the wash of notes, the green waves
breaking and taking us
into the current like starburst

How many stars need you wish?

What I Remember Most is Everything

Blue Gum Eucalyptus

Some say you are a beautiful mistake
an invasive species so native now

we don't remember you arriving
during the Gold Rush years

how you survived and spread
your roots then anchored hills

providing a home for monarchs
and other migrants heading west

I remember once when I'll be walking
in the foothills, the sky pale peacock blue

with a spray of poppies in the June grass
near the grove where you'll be waiting

rustling your leaves and peeling limbs,
making woody-sweet perfume—a cure

like the balm from Gilead—for wings
of the butterfly and the hands of a girl.

COUNTERPOINTS

Color, Memory

That now
is
history

as mist
felt
not fact

as wind
swept
not tracked

sequined
as a glint
of sun

hidden
in a face
now gone

hues
spiraling
past

so time
might bend
her arms

around you.

Speak, Color

i.

Color as memory, a sinuous spurt
squeezed from the tube
and brushed between steps,
the lull between breath
spinning her hair round a hurricane's eye

absorbing the sounds and the shapes
traces of faces and place
the tender and tremulous times,
her threads running through
back to the start.

ii.

Color as context, the days are textual
such a sensual parting, and the theatre
is standing room only, and by the exit
he sees only grey lemons, while she sees through

the door, a girl practicing how to walk in darkness
and off she goes into the woods, knowing
everything and nothing, with a network of nerves
and a brush filled with yellow paint

to meet the blockage of branches head on—
a migration of sensations.

iii.

Maybe we would all be better off
with a fat slice of synesthesia—

let letters press in colors
set to the contours of each still mind
let cerulean rule, let persian green run sublime
against a saucy red eyelid

let Hockney's flaming *A Closer Grand Canyon*
sixty canvases strong carry us
let the blue rain of the brain in
let us pray—*to light.*

iv.

An increase in color visually reduces its distance—

try to pick grapes with the farmworkers
in van Gogh's *Red Vineyard*
try to sit in his yellow chair
try on that yellow raincoat hanging

try to play the red notes
on Kandinsky's white keyboard

try on Nabokov's eye-shut-kind of visual
where the objective, optical replica lives—is
in natural colors—a little g h o s t.

COMPOSITIONS

Red Square

> *If one says "Red" (the name of a color)*
> *and there are 50 people listening*
> *it can be expected that there will be 50 reds in their minds…*
> *—Josef Albers*

Say green and you will see green
in your own way,
hot, warm or cool and dependent
on so many things.

I stare hard and long at a red square
and overcome by redness, look away,
to see the sum of all the others
waiting patiently as you—

rods, cones and retinas ready
like our plans

to take yellow and blue to make
her complement.

Green yes, but new.

Can you stake your colors to these words?
These worlds?

Dear Matisse

I never thanked you personally,

although I named my dog after you,
although he's dying—

for all the windows you painted
so we can see from any chair
in every room

that it is true what you said—

that you only painted the difference
between things—

    palms and pomegranates
    pineapples and red walls

what we see beyond the sill of our eyes,
what *gives*

You once said you wouldn't mind being
a vermilion goldfish
and I believe you—

looking out through watered glass
how gills move to the desire for

condensation of sensation.

Artist and Goldfish

plus 30 more paintings by Henri Matisse

Woman sitting on a balcony with violet stockings
        and a green parasol . Woman in a purple coat .
        Violinist at the window .

Sketch for music . The piano lesson . Dance .
        The Egyptian curtain .
        Large red interior . Harmony in red .

The pineapple . Basket of oranges .
        Pewter jug, lemons and chair .
        Silence living in houses .

Studio under the eaves . The painter and his model .
        The blue blouse . Blue nude .
        Blue eyes . The blue window .

By the sea . The painter's family .
        The parakeet and the mermaid .
        The swimmer in the aquarium .

The young sailor . The yellow curtain .
        Bathers by a river . Bathers with a turtle .
        Goldfish . Conversation .

The open window .

van Gogh's Red Vineyard

A ten-minute walk from Red Square in Moscow
the sun was so hot, the sky so yellow
the cerulean skin of the trees so real
I just stood
between the red vines and grasses.

Do they have water? They're crouched low
and bent like bales in long skirts
picking grapes. A wagon, a horse waits.

A dark figure stands off to the right
in the distance, ominous.
He is counting something. Them?

"Nyet, nyet," the guard says. "Step away."

I took your photograph at the Pushkin then
the only painting sold in your lifetime
for 400 francs to another painter, Anna Boch.

Sun fades the objects in our hands, but not
the flame remembered.

Road with Cypress and Star

plus 27 more paintings by Vincent van Gogh

The man with the pipe . Pair of old shoes .
> Postman Joseph Roulin . Thistles .
> Cypresses with two female figures .

Poets garden with round clipped shrub and weeping
> tree . Two girls . Two white butterflies .
> Blossoming pear tree .

Self portrait with straw hat . Two cut sunflowers .
> Fields under a stormy sky . Green corn .
> Crows on the cornfields .

Two poplars on a road through the hills . Trees
> in a field on a sunny day . Women picking
> olives . The church near Auvers .

Stone bench in the garden of Saint-Paul Hospital .
> The nurse . Four sunflowers gone
> to seed . Wild roses .

Self portrait with bandaged ear and pipe .
> Ears of wheat . Sheaves of wheat .
> Undergrowth .

Wheat stacks with reaper .

The Water Lilies at Giverny

Slip through the surface
let loose your lolling roots, fleshy flower *Nymphaea*

turn on your back and open your face
to the circular sun.

He is looking down into the sky
gently poking with his paint, a touch of pink

leaning over the grassy bank
brush to reed to water-petal-lip.

He is looking and nothing
will stop him from looking—not his hunger nor rain,

not his dimming, cataract eyes—nothing until
he has lit every mirrored mouth.

Is that why we are so ethereal? Detached
from description?

Lilies glazed until we become
the illusion of the endless whole

on and on, across the pewtered pond.

Portal in the Sun

plus 27 more paintings by Claude Monet

Grainstacks in the sunlight morning effect .
        The haystack . The water lily pond .
        Yellow and lilac water lilies .

The blue row boat . The pink skiff .
        Fog effect . Three trees in grey weather .
        Yellow irises with pink cloud .

The Japanese bridge . The strollers .
        Springtime through the branches .
        Sunlight effect under the poplars .

The house seen from the rose garden .
        Women in the garden . Luncheon
on the grass . Camille at the window .

An interior after dinner . Corner of a studio .
        Self portrait with a beret . Portrait of a girl .
        Bouquet of mallows .

Branch of lemons . Lighthouse at the hospice .
        Under the pine trees at the end of the day .
        Thunderstorms .

The landing state .

Two Blue Riders

In Munich, you pulled on your riding boots—

the horse was restless
and I listened
by the stable door
as you rode off, *The Blue Rider*

spurring the rhythm in paint
across the green meadow
to the blue mountain
composing the colors of sound

objects left but the subject remained
storm and stars passed
shape became space
the improvisation.

In Bern, the cows carried their bells—

over the green hills
and I listened
munching sweet grass
while you were choosing

bread for lunch
then cleaned the house
and fed the cat, began to paint
shades of night violet and gold

your *Separation in the Evening*
drew two opposing arrows
(unequal) in the banded sky
what space between them?

In Dessau, at the Bauhaus where you both taught—

after the Great War
after you brought us *White Sound*
The Light and So Much Else
together you will walk home from work

pour two cups of tea
kick off your shoes beside the hearth
sit down for your evening conversation
concerning the soul of painting

outside: earth and sky
the horses waiting.

The Blue Rider (1903) / White Sound (1908)
  by Wassily Kandinsky

Separation in the Evening (1922) / The Light and So Much Else (1931)
  by Paul Klee

Composition with Saints

plus 27 more paintings by Wassily Kandinsky

The blue rider . In the black square .
    Black lines .
    In the forest . Small pleasures .

Trumpet blowing rider . Twilight .
    Blue mountain . Untitled .
    Three riders .

Sketchbook . Sky blue . Six
    female nudes standing .
    Painting with white border .

English garden in Munich .
    Early hour . Several circles .
    Yellow-red-blue .

The cow . Cossacks . Cliffs .
    Storm bell .
    Landscape with church .

Angel of the last judgment .
    White sound .
    Hollow energy .

Heavy between light .

Separation in the Evening

plus 30 more paintings by Paul Klee

Houses near the gravel pit . Place signs .
    Six species . Flowers in stone .
    This flower wishes to fade .

Cat and bird . Red balloon . Full moon .
    Still life with thistle bloom . Rocks at night .
    Miraculous landing . New harmony .

Portrait of Mrs. P in the South . Possessed
    girl . A young lady's adventure . Portrait
    of a man . Glass façade . Characters in yellow .

Before the Blitz . Growth of the night plants .
    Remembrance of a garden . The messenger
    of autumn . Ravaged land . Revolving house .

Hesitation . Struck from the list . Death
    and fire . Rising sun .
    Cosmic composition .

The light and so much else .

Mourning Breakfast

Breakfast of the Birds (1934) by Gabriele Münter

Could I share breakfast with you
this cold and snow-filled morning?
I'm behind your shoulder on the left
watching them with you, six brown birds
with muffled beaks, branches bowed
and stirring in the mottled light
hung like fog against the window.

Coffee and cream, pitcher and plate
on your left. You off-center slightly right.
Heavy mauve drapes parted
down the middle like your hair (maybe)
but I can't see your face looking out at winter.

Bread and cheese untouched, no knife
in sight. Right arm smudged at the elbow
so I can't tell if you are eating or grieving—
a bent arm lifting hand to mouth
or stiff-limbed staring out, snowcapped
like a white plate of crumbs.
It's 1934 and turning dark so early.

Girl with Red Bow

plus 31 more paintings by Gabriele Münter

Portrait of a young woman . Listening .
    Bouquet with oak leaves .
    Little green house . Future .

Garden gate . Buttercups and mimosa .
    The yellow house . The blue mountain .
    A lake in the mountains .

Towards evening . Fisherman's house .
    Avenue in the Park of St. Cloud .
    Road in multicolored October .

Still life with queen . Friend .
    Self-portrait in front of an easel .
    Abstract composition . Meditation .

Landscape with white wall . Interior .
    Still life with figures . Dahlias .
    Breakfast of the birds .

The Russian's house . Reflecting .
    In the room . Flowers and shadows .
    After tea . Black path .

Dark still life .

Morandi Still Life: Cat and Five Objects

All those years ago in Bologna,
your studio a still life

two ordinary windows
one wood table, a world of objects—

I am thinking, watching my white cat
perched on the window sill

how perfect a model she would make
poised between two of your cream pitchers

patient as marble in surround sound

set to the left of the bottle, bowl and tin box on the table
the six of them snug in pearled light.

You said—*nothing can be more abstract than reality*

So how can we believe what we see?

Natura Morta

plus 1,341 more paintings by Georgio Morandi

Still life .

The Work of Gray

Black and White stand firm at their poles apart
between lives Gray
so caught and often not heard above their shouting

barely breaking darkness

she rises early to cut out on her own (on tiptoe)
scales the backyard fence with Fog
and races through the field to your screen door

comes inside to hide from them awhile

holds on tight to that sinking feeling
(her greatest Fear)
that Black will take her when she is least looking

pull her deep, make her invisible

she tiptoes to the front door and peers out
afraid she'll go blind
staring hard at the white sun.

It's not fair the way the work of Gray never ends—

Let her Rest.

I Was So Small I Saw So Much

I walked in the tea on my spoon
lighter than you in your cup

my tears had no color
but I could see the edge

of the ocean opaque as milk
but more blue in the center

the way more color brings us
closer to the lips of what we love.

The Green Fuse

> *The force that through the green fuse drives the flower*
> *Drives my green age...*
> —Dylan Thomas

For your eyes I ask for
a diamond sidewalk with dirt paths

birch and burdock leaves
with their drying curls of lace

and desert walks in tumbleweed

lay down what you own, there is only the trying

Her hands could read violets
she could walk a straight line

to match the pace of her seeing
late for the green light racing home

but not too late

lay down what you own, there is only the flying

I was fully dressed with shoes on
by the front door

with a brush and a green flower
and a free hour
ready to go anywhere

TRAVEL

Two Suitcases

Let us be the last of the toting tribe—
full of paper, spice and shells
what thumbs can touch like plums feed

needle-pricked and juiced, casting
our names in the cow-licked grass, serving
what is actually, not virtually the case

our bodies lugged and stuffed with
walking shoes, maps and paints
no electronic voyage for us

we'll shuffle through spangled stations
our clasps snapping, crisp as dried twigs breaking
our souls not lost or mistaken

we'll fill our sides with eggs and seeds
some flower buds and sweet berries
each specimen sugared on the tongue

and when we finally reach our destination
we'll find ourselves—
sprung

Yukon Gold

The best I ever ate
was baked
before boarding
north of Bologna

a packed train
near midnight
six girls traveling
bunched tight

rain coming hard
against glass
rocked
the train's trespass

heading northwest
when Marianne pulled
her magic trick
out of a burlap bag

a dozen wrapped hot
in silver swiftly passed
Yukon Golds
fingered and eaten

just like that
sitting on backpacks
safe in the middle
of a journey

see past the fast windows
the potato fields plowed
by our great-grandfathers
flowering white

still hungry
amid the rumble
remembering
no raincoats

no matter
the green rain
and Ireland
waiting.

Sunday in Sicily

> *Wonder—is not precisely Knowing*
> *And not precisely Knowing not—*
> *—Emily Dickinson*

I watched a long-stemmed man
selling newspapers from his car
one Sunday morning in Sicily
on the road to Siracusa heading south

enormous bundles in every window
tied like leaves and bunched
till they were almost bursting
and I noticed then

the open trunk
revealed another man
this one moderately-sized
a black cap on his head

and he was dead, I thought

I bought the paper, *La Repubblica*
and the newspaper man
wearing grey
fished out my change

then woke him up
the groggy man
who held in his hand
a plastic cup

and when I looked again
I glimpsed them—
seven yellow roses in his other hand—
he gave me one, *prego*

molte grazie, I said
and slowly walked away

the newspaper and the flower
died that day
but I found something else to save
I call the wonder stone.

Saint Petersburg

That winter there was circus dusk
the taste of sour black bread and stars,
an eye cup filled with warm saltwater
in a small school at sunset, silent
except for the fallow field, snow melt
and a nurse who happened by
who took my eye gently in her hands
speaking softly in Russian, and I saw
in the comfort of solitude how
one warm thing leads to another,
the fleck removed in the gold window
as she washed my face like a moraine.

The Spanish Steps

the day was oyster white
the sun all cumin and curry

leaning out the fourth floor
window, streets steaming

two lovers dressed in Technicolor
prance across the marble steps

reciting verse with tinctured tongues
their music rising warm the way

color creates spice and sweat
and sometimes glazes love

Black Forest Walk

The eye sees darkness
the way a forest
swallows her trees
ankles to knees,
the inky black rising
like a new moon night.
If walking alone,
hold your own hands
and use your third eye
as a scorching torch
to fill the mind's
pool with light—
a frisson vision,
the truest kind.

What Light Can Do

If you only have one cake   make space

If you only have one day   make space

If you have a dark color   make space

If you have unbearable grief   make space

All you bring   give light   to carry.

Munich Was Radiant

> ...over the festive plazas and white columned temples...
> spanned a heaven shimmering as blue silk
> —Thomas Mann

In Munich, we met Kandinsky
on the white walls
of the Lenbachhaus Museum
in all his glory, his sun
cutting through paint like stained glass in cathedrals
we thought *this is how to live*

and carried the shards of color
out the door with us
and later leaned against graffiti
on the Berlin Wall
before passing through
Checkpoint Charlie

a grey day in a drizzled sun
and in a park in East Berlin
found only old grey men
wearing grey and playing chess
and it was quiet except
for the rooks and queens

and we continued on, propelled
across borders
moving ahead by feeling
without knowing

without seeing where
we might next be going

and we threw green stones
into white clouds on the lake
and the lake was citrine
along its rim where opposites meet
and we met others that summer
and were like young birds

and then it was time
dear girl
a stranger said,
you will need to find the words
like a bird pinning worms
and we flew home to San Francisco.

Knitting in the Dark

The hour before she brings morning

to the house of wonder

she breathes a violet breath that holds

before advancing—

      as a gutter drips rain slow

      as a room fills slow with filtered light

      as a knitter picks and pulls a strand of memory

makes woolen wings

      as real as the leaf

      on this window.

List of Things Left I Will Come Back For

fog on a hill

city lights

piano keys

cup of tea

mangos

violets

white cat

watercolor dress

bowl of tangerines

green flower

water glass

salted light

baked potatoes

bus ticket

backpack

eucalyptus

Desire Path

for Matti

Words
will follow you
like a dog
down the street
will be waiting
at the window
for you to come
home to fill
the bowl
with water
wherever you go.
Think about
a treat without
a shape and give
it bone.
Take the shape
and ink it
in small letters.
Shake and paint
the colors
in the grass,
pressed as
your gold paws
now white
make.

Sparring Time

Time stands in the center of the ring.
Shadow boxing with all comers.

Thick thumbs.
    Empty mind.
        Plumbed heart.

Let's die knowing something.

Nothing lost trying.
What keeps us looking?

Punch.
    Blow.
        Side-step.

Thrown in the corner.
Up against the rope swinging.
Bell ringing.

Every thing divisible.

Pieces of us everywhere.

We Made the Rain

When the eyes could no longer paint
we called all colors to the field
set down our canvas
and stones as paperweights
then stood and poured
to hear the sounds of color

We made the rain.

In flowered light // white
a purple chirp // a madder rap
a ping of cinnamon // crimson
the eek of green
a hoot of blue // a coo
the pant of tan
and a thousand others
spoke their colors

We soaked our skin and turned
our faces to the falling drops
and smelled the summer ending
knowing the painting time
was now the time to wait
for the innerness of things.

We made the rain.

RETURN

Climbing the Seven Hills

Russian Hill > Telegraph Hill > Twin Peaks > Mount Sutro > Rincon Hill > Mount Davidson > Nob Hill

You
can start
anywhere, like here
climbing one in San Francisco
the fog at each throat thick, motionless
against emotion but moving, dressed and pressing
up Russian Hill, pausing step by step to jump the cracks
in sidewalks hopscotched past but not chosen, so let's go

Tap
tap your toes
up Telegraph, the steady
march, the notion of shadow, how slow
time moves before we see her lashes grow, the baby
with the cereal bowl who will become the girl balancing
pink cake boxes, who will drop them and become the mother
calling her children, pulling joy like teeth sometimes, so let's go

Drip
drip like fog
hiking up Twin Peaks
everlasting and Mission blue
like the endangered butterflies flying low
lupine to lupine past the hiss-hiss hustle of the bus
shuttling up and up, drawing and discarding passengers
carrying packages with histories imagined in passing, so let's go

Digest
the stakes up
Mount Sutro, past the man
cooking artichokes and lemons
in the silver window, who is drumming
his pan with a wooden spoon, the notes falling free
as salt shaking, as free as the kisses his daughter blows
puckered to the smiling boy from the peeling sill, so let's go

Push
on and up
belted in mist
through the grove of blue
gum eucalyptus and turn northeast
to see downtown the violet-veiled towers
built on Rincon near Folsom and just south of Market
and the girders of the Bay Bridge spanning the way, so let's go

Press
on up Mount
Davidson picking
huckleberries in Pacific reeds
to the cross on the peak and glimpse below
the griddled streets and scrub undercover hiding
her feet and the glass sun spackling the sky's mirrored towers
as we count the bay's container ships like silicon chips, so let's go

Choose
between views
as the girl, in pursuit
of herself, climbs the seventh hill
and will find herself back in the apartment
on the corner of Taylor and Sacramento, sweeping
the kitchen floor in her black boots as the earth quakes
and she reaches for the light and her backpack and says, let's go.

Notes on the Artists

The collection was inspired by the decade I lived in San Francisco during my twenties and is an ode of sorts to the city and the artists I loved most then. Many of the featured artists experienced synesthesia, the neurological condition in which letters, numbers or musical notes are associated with specific colors or other sensations. In the collaged "painting title" poems (each period separating one painting from another) the titles are arranged in a sequence that aims to tell a story about the artist. Featured artists are listed below in order of appearance.

Wassily Kandinsky (1866–1944) called for a spiritual revolution in painting in his groundbreaking work, *Concerning the Spiritual in Art,* in which he also discussed the psychology and language of color and form. His work inspired "Two Blue Riders" and "Composition with Saints." Kandinsky had synesthesia.

Wayne Thiebaud (b. 1920) inspired "California City," composed from a selection of his landscape paintings of San Francisco and the Sacramento River Delta.

David Hockney (b. 1937) inspired "Pacific Coast Highway & Santa Monica," composed from a selection of his California landscape paintings. Hockney has synesthesia.

Vladimir Nabokov (1899–1977) and his memoir *Speak, Memory* inspired "Color, Memory" and "Speak, Color." Nabokov had synesthesia.

Josef Albers (1888–1976) demonstrated how the perception of color is dependent on its context in his seminal work, *Interaction of Color*. Albers inspired "Red Square."

Henri Matisse (1869–1954) inspired "Dear Matisse" and "Artist and Goldfish."

Vincent van Gogh (1853–1890) inspired "van Gogh's Red Vineyard" and "Road with Cypress and Star." van Gogh may have had synesthesia.

Claude Monet (1840–1926) painted the water lilies at Giverny for more than thirty years, despite severe cataracts he developed late in life. Monet inspired "The Water Lilies at Giverny" and Portal in the Sun."

Paul Klee (1879–1940) inspired "Two Blue Riders" and "Separation in the Evening." The former reflects the friendship of Kandinsky and Klee, both members of *Der Blaue Reiter* who also taught together at the Bauhaus in the 1920s.

Gabriele Münter (1877–1962), another member of *Der Blaue Reiter*, inspired "Mourning Breakfast" and "The Red Bow."

Georgio Morandi (1890–1964) inspired "Morandi Still Life: Cat and Five Objects" and "Natura Morta."

Acknowledgements

Special thanks to fellow writers and poets Jean Blakeman, Beth Filson, Libby Maxey, Rebecca Olander and Adin Thayer for invaluable feedback, support and the gift of Wednesday poetry nights.

Thanks to the members of the Florence Poets Society for providing such a welcoming and supportive community of poets. Thanks to Linda McCullough Moore and the Saturday morning writers group; also thanks to Carol Edelstein. A special thanks to fellow poet Marian Kent for encouragement and support.

Love and thanks to my children Kelly, William and Samuel for touching everything.

And love and thanks beyond words to John, for being there in Berkeley at the end of that decade, to walk into the next and all the rest together.

About the Author

Sharon Tracey is a writer and editor who has enjoyed a varied career as an environmentalist, program manager, policy analyst and communications director. Her work has appeared in *Naugatuck River Review, Silkworm, The Skinny Poetry Journal* and other publications. This is her first full-length collection of poems. She received her Master's degree from the University of California Berkeley and lives in Amherst, Massachusetts.

www.ingramcontent.com/pod-product-compliance
Lightning Source LLC
Chambersburg PA
CBHW060359050426
42449CB00009B/1810